DISCUSSION PAPER 69

THE CHALLENGE OF SUB-REGIONAL SECURITY IN WEST AFRICA
The Case of the 2006 ECOWAS Convention
on Small Arms and Light Weapons

LINDA DARKWA

NORDISKA AFRIKAINSTITUTET, UPPSALA 2011

Indexing terms:
West Africa
Weapons
Small arms
Armament
Disarmament
Arms transfers
Cross-border trade
Informal sector
Organized crime
Regional security
Regional cooperation
Post-conflict reconstruction

The opinions expressed in this volume are those of the author and do not necessarily reflect the views of Nordiska Afrikainstitutet.

Language checking: Peter Colenbrander
ISSN 1104-8417
ISBN 978-91-7106-710-4
© The author and Nordiska Afrikainstitutet 2011
Production: Byrå4
Print on demand, Lightning Source UK Ltd.

Contents

Foreword 5

Introduction 7

Controlling Small Arms and Light Weapons: Some Conceptual Considerations
Licit versus illicit weapons: definitional clarification 9

Controlling SALW Proliferation: Some Critical Considerations 9

The Proliferation of SALW: Global and West African Perspectives The Global Scene 11

West Africa: Insights into SALW Proliferation in the Sub-Region 13

Demand and Supply of SALW in West Africa 18

ECOWAS and SALW Proliferation: From Moratorium to Convention 20

Insights into the ECOWAS Convention on SALW 22

Implementing the ECOWAS SALW Convention: The Challenges 27

Conclusion 29

Recommendations..29

Bibliography..33

Foreword

This Discussion Paper critically examines the nature and effectiveness of the 2006 ECOWAS Convention on Small Arms and Light Weapons (SALW), their Ammunition and Other Related Materials, and the policies of the governments of ECOWAS member states in curbing illegal arms transfers and facilitating sub-regional peace, security and development. The paper provides an overview of the global discourse on and efforts at limiting the scourge of SALW proliferation. It then pays particular attention to the background and evolution of collective efforts in West Africa to curb the menace of SALW proliferation based on the recognised linkages between illegal arms flows, human suffering and intra-regional conflict, violence and cross-border and transnational criminal activities, such as arms, human and drug trafficking, illegal mining and crude oil theft. It also places the convention in the context of West Africa's peace and security architecture, one of the most advanced in Africa, based on the 1993 revised ECOWAS treaty, its various protocols, particularly the 1999 Protocol on Conflict Prevention, Management and Resolution, Peacekeeping and Security, and the common African position on the UN Programme of Action on SALW. The paper then provides a critical examination of ECOWAS's efforts at curbing SALW proliferation, focusing on the relevant institutions and mechanisms involved. This includes examination of the ECOWAS Small Arms Control Programme (ECOSAP), certain provisions of the convention and the challenges of implementing decisions and policies. The author concludes by making important recommendations to strengthen the convention and sharpen its effectiveness in responding to the challenges that proliferation of illicit SALW pose to West Africa's development, peace and security.

Cyril Obi
Senior Researcher
The Nordic Africa Institute

Introduction

West Africa is at a critical juncture in its socioeconomic and political development. On the one hand, it is well endowed in terms of natural resources, strategic location and large market and has great potential for development and peace, while on the other, it is confronted with a number of challenges that render its rather fragile institutions and post-conflict societies vulnerable to political instability, economic crisis and violent conflict. One such threat is the proliferation of small arms and light weapons (SALW) in the sub-region, as is evident from the outbreak and aftermath of civil wars in Liberia, Sierra Leone, Guinea Bissau and Côte d'Ivoire, the Tuareg revolts in Niger and Mali and the insurgency in Nigeria's Niger Delta.

Although the sub-region has one of Africa's most sophisticated peace and security architectures (Obi 2009: 119), it still faces formidable intra-regional security challenges. Of note are the threats posed by the connections between the proliferation of SALW, violent conflict and the activities of transnational criminal networks operating in the region and peace, security and development in West Africa.

These networks are well established in some West African countries, which are regarded as hubs for global criminal networks that engage in illegal activities such as drug and human trafficking, arms proliferation, illegal mining of minerals, cross-border crime and smuggling and piracy. There are also reports of some criminals successfully infiltrating the highest echelons of security and border control agencies in some countries in the sub-region. The infiltration is particularly prevalent in countries with weak structures and limited capacities for promoting the rule of law (UNDOC 2010a, b). With their connections to government officials, these cross-border networks are able to undermine law enforcement efforts and operate with impunity.

In some countries, high levels of unemployment, weak governance and porous borders have rendered the sub-region vulnerable to transnational and violent cross-border crimes. In its 2010 annual report, the United Nations Office on Drugs and Crime asserts that:

> West Africa is a paradise for organized crime, offering ideal conditions for trafficking contraband: a strategic location, porous borders, weak governance, widespread poverty and extensive corruption. As a result, criminals and insurgents are exploiting the region. West Africa serves as a transit point between Latin America and Europe for US$ 1 billion-worth in cocaine, as a destination for counterfeit medicines and toxic waste, and as a source of stolen natural resources, particularly oil. Human trafficking, whether for forced labour or sexual exploitation, also occurs in the region. (UNODC 2010b: 31)

The foregoing scenario provides a rather unflattering perspective on the context for SALW proliferation. State monopoly over the use of force is countered by persons with unauthorised access to small arms, who are often part of organised criminal netorks (BBC 2008a, 2008b). In the Niger Delta region, insurgent militias have used illegally obtained SALW to kidnap oil company personnel, sabotage oil pipelines and engage in the transnational trade in stolen crude oil. Clearly, what began as an agitation for the equitable distribution of the oil wealth of the Niger Delta has taken on a criminal character.

These rebels challenged the state's monopoly of the use of force by engaging government security forces in pitched battle and attacking oil company assets, causing Nigeria to lose almost 30 per cent of its daily oil production and expected oil revenues at the peak of the crisis. During the disarmament programme that followed the amnesty to Niger Delta insurgents in 2009, hundreds of small arms and light weapons were surrendered by ex-rebels to the Nigerian authorities. Since then, relative calm has returned to the oil-rich Niger Delta, and oil production has returned to pre-conflict levels.

Considerable attention is paid in this paper to the threats posed by the proliferation of SALW in the sub-region and the efforts of the Economic Community of West African States (ECOWAS) through its 2006 Convention on Small Arms and Light Weapons, their Ammunition and Other Related Materials (ECOWAS 2006), to resolve the problem. It critically examines the nature and effectiveness of the ECOWAS convention and the policies of ECOWAS member-state governments in curbing illegal arms transfers and facilitating sub-regional security.

This discussion paper contributes to the ongoing debate on SALW control in West Africa in the hope of providing deeper insights into and data on the connections between effective small arms control, security and sustainable development in the sub-region. It is divided into five sections, including this introduction. The next section provides a conceptual exploration of certain issues related to the regulation and control of illegal SALW flows. The third section analyses global and regional perspectives on the proliferation of SALW and the measures taken to control the problem. In section four, deeper insights are provided into the provisions of ECOWAS convention and the extent to which they have been able to address the security challenges posed by SALW. The conclusion includes recommendations to enable the convention to effectively curb the menace of SALW proliferation in West Africa.

Controlling Small Arms and Light Weapons: Some Conceptual Considerations

Licit versus illicit weapons: definitional clarification

The licit and illicit dichotomy in arms proliferation is problematic, given the fluidity of the two terms. It is a function of legal interpretation/status, which may depend on a change of location, designation, jurisdiction and ownership. Licit firearms are those that are (a) manufactured or assembled in conformity with the laws of the country of manufacture and (b) procured and distributed in accordance with national, regional and international laws. Illicit firearms, on the other hand, are those (a) manufactured or assembled in violation of national laws and (b) procured and distributed in contravention of national, regional and international laws. Distribution of arms includes sales by states and commercial entities as well as transfers by states. An arm is licit only if it meets the triple criteria of legal manufacture, procurement and distribution in its totality. Therefore, if arms are legally manufactured, legally procured, but illegally distributed, they lose their licit status.

Flowing from this, the classification of an arm as licit or illicit is a product of origin, destination and use. It is important to clarify that the function to which a weapon is put does not render it illicit. Thus, a licit weapon used in the commission of an illegal act does not change the status of the weapon. This calls for a specific set of coordinated and enforceable rules, separate from what is required for dealing with illicit weapons, to guard against such occurrences.

Controlling SALW Proliferation: Some Critical Considerations

Small arms have multiple functions: they can be used in the provision of security by the state and authorised individuals, to symbolise authority in some traditional governance structures and serve as status symbols connoting power, wealth and maturity in some cultures. They are, however, also used to induce fear and commit crimes. Irrespective of their use, small arms can be lethal if improperly handled. Owing to the multiple uses of small arms, strategies for the regulation of access, acquisition and use must be properly designed to guarantee their effectiveness.

The control of licit weapons aims at providing safeguards against their falling into the hands of unauthorised persons as well as preventing their unauthorised use by authorised persons. Controlling illicit proliferation, on the other hand, is geared at preventing such weapons from being accessible and available to all persons. In other words, licit weapons are to be controlled by putting measures in place assigning responsibility for their acquisition, possession and use, whilst illicit weapons are to be completely banned.

There was considerable state control on the production and supply of small arms prior to and during the Cold War. However, the level of control fell dramatically in the post-Cold War era. According to Naylor (2001), two main reasons may account for this development – the inability of major powers to influence the supply side of the arms trade and the ability of non-state actors to access and purchase weapons hitherto inaccessible to them. Naylor surmises that during the Cold War there were strict controls on the production and distribution of weapons and "countries came to agree that the business of arms manufacturing, where not already state-owned, would be state-regulated and that they (China remains the one big exception) would issue no export licences unless the would-be purchaser produced an end-user certificate …" (2010: 213).

According to Naylor, since the US and the former Soviet Union were the world's major manufacturers and suppliers of weapons, they could excercise control over producers and, as such, led the control efforts. The occasional violations of control mechanisms were exceptions to the norm. During the Cold War, the superpowers provided their allies and satellite states with weapons from their stocks either as gifts or on generous credit terms. At the end of the Cold War, the allied states became geopolitically irrelevant to the two superpowers. Consequently, the supply of weapons was considerably reduced and, in some instances, completely stopped.

The end of the Cold War, however, saw the opening of a Pandora's box in several countries. Governments that had been able to fend off the opposition suddenly found themselves in fierce battles with non-state actors. The need to dispose of Cold War weapon surpluses and expansion of production capacity led to a glut of weapons in arms-producing countries. Consequently the "desire to promote arms exports as a means of earning foreign exchange" (Naylor 2001: 216) resulted in the availability of weapons to non-state actors.

This new access to weapons provided a new impetus to groups in opposition to the governments of their countries and arguably helped to transform erstwhile latent tensions into armed violence in some countries. With profit as the main driving force, states were willing to overlook weapons control regimes in order to promote sales and maximise returns. Consequently, although the end-user certificate was supposed to be "a pledge by relevant officials in the purchasing country that the arms were intended solely for the use of that country's military forces and would not be transferred to third parties without permission of the country of origin" (Naylor 2010: 212), this practice was severely undermined in a number of ways by states.

Thus, government control over the distribution of weapons dwindled considerably in the immediate post-Cold War era, even though there were still strict controls on manufacture. In other words, in the main the strict controls on the production of most arms did not extend to their supply and distribution. For instance, with the exception of Guinea-Bissau, which fought a liberation war, independence in West Africa was largely a negotiated settlement and devoid of the armed violence of other regions. Secondly, West Africa was not a target for the proxy wars of the superpowers and did not witness the large-scale distribution of arms to Cold War satellite states. It can therefore be assumed that the majority of arms in circulation in the sub-region are relatively new and a product of post-Cold War dynamics.

Broadcasts of the carnage of the 1990s from Eastern Europe to West Africa jolted the world. The images of destruction and human suffering in armed conflicts brought about by the irresponsible use of SALW sent a grave message to the world. In addition, there was increasing awareness of the role played by SALW in the perpetration of other crimes. Thus, in 2001, as the embers of armed conflict were dying around the world, global and regional efforts were made to tackle small arms proliferation globally.

There have been a number of such efforts. They include the United Nations Programme of Action (UNPoA), the UN Protocol against the Illicit Manufacturing of and Trafficking in Firearms, their Parts and Components and Ammunition (the Firearms Protocol), the International Tracing Instrument (ITI), the Nairobi Declaration for the Great Lakes and Horn of Africa, the Inter-American Convention against the Illicit Manufacturing of and Trafficking in Firearms, Ammunition, Explosives and Other Related Materials and the Organisation of Security and Cooperation in Europe (OSCE) Document on Small Arms and Light Weapons. All are useful developments in the control of small arms proliferation. This consensus on the need for control gave increased momentum to the fight against SALW proliferation at all levels as a critical element in the quest for sustainable global peace and development.

The Proliferation of SALW: Global and West African Perspectives
The Global Scene

The aim of global arms control measures was twofold: regulate legitimate access, acquisition and use and ban access, acquisition and use by unauthorised persons. By instituting processes and mechanisms to verify and document the source, channels of transportation and destination of arms, governments enhanced responsibility through transparency by making available sufficient information to ascertain who has what, from where and for what.

In theory, arms control efforts are predicated on the assumption that governments legitimately represent states and are endowed with responsibility to protect and guarantee the security of the state and its people. In democratic states, this assumption stems from the social contract between rulers and ruled that vests authority and the monopoly of the use of force in the government in exchange for responsible governance and security.

This assumption is, however, put to the test when governments exploit their authority and use legally acquired small arms for illegitimate purposes. Investing a government with the authority to regulate arms acquisition and use assumes the government has the authority to govern. This is a fair assumption, but could be contentious especially when an incumbent president refuses to leave office at the end of his/her term and unleashes the state's security machinery to create insecurity in the state. In such instances, when non-coercive measures fail to yield the desired result, it becomes difficult to ensure the will of the people will prevail when the tools for forcible removal are vested in the oppressor.

According to a UN-led study, "small arms have a disproportionate impact – while accounting for only one-fifth of the global arms trade, they maim and kill far more than any other conventional weapons" (IRIN 2006). The increasing use of SALW in most of the world's conflicts and crime, with global trade (in SALW) valued at over US$ 1 billion annually, coupled with the fact that these weapons are relatively easy to use, readily available and difficult to regulate, has caught the attention of many observers. However, it was not until 2001 that global attempts were made to tackle the growing challenge of SALW proliferation to peace, security and development.

This intervention was in the form of the UN's Firearms Protocol, which made illegal transfers of SALW a crime. The Firearms Protocol was directed at addressing SALW proliferation in a holistic manner: it was designed to regulate and control the manufacture and supply of firearms, their parts and components as well as ammunition.

Also, in July 2001, a conference on the illicit trade in SALW in all its aspects was organised by the UN. Participants at the conference adopted UNPoA to eradicate illicit proliferation. Unlike the Firearms Protocol, UNPoA was agreed by consensus. Although UNPoA recommended measures for member states to take to ensure small arms control, it did not provide for binding sanctions against those violating the agreement. Thus, the global effort to rein-in illegal trafficking in SALW has achieved mixed results at best, or at worst failed to eliminate this highly profitable illegal trade in SALW in a rapidly globalising world, prompting the efforts that led UN member states to agree in 2009 on the need for a strong(er) global Arms Trade Treaty (ATT).

As Wallacher and Harang (2011: 6) in their well-researched report note in relation to the place of SALW in the debates on the ATT, there is a "common understanding that proliferation of conventional arms contributes to human rights violations, breaches of international humanitarian law, to intensifying and prolonging armed conflict, and threatens national and regional security". Their observations have deeper significance in those regions of the world where SALW have become weapons of choice for warlords, criminal networks (drug and human trafficking, piracy, mineral and oil smuggling) and other conflict actors, resulting in immense human suffering, death, destruction and insecurity. They assume even more significance in national and local contexts where the destructive impact of SALW proliferation is directly experienced. This situation makes it more compelling that global efforts and discourses be harmonised with ongoing processes at the local, national and regional levels. In the context of this paper, the extent to which ECOWAS has taken proactive initiatives to tackle the scourge of SALW proliferation in the sub-region, and their success or otherwise and how they connect with or reflect ongoing efforts and debates at the global level will be critically examined.

West Africa: Insights into SALW Proliferation in the Sub-Region

In West Africa, there are three main sources of SALW – extant stocks that are recycled; new imports, which may include brand-new weapons and ammunition as well as used weapons recycled from outside the sub-region; and local craft production in countries of the sub-region. The proliferation of SALWs in West Africa is traceable to the mid-to-late 1960s, when authoritarian, repressive and exclusionary policies employed by post-independence leaders in the name of nation-building in highly diverse societies led to discontent, protests among segments of their populations and, in extreme cases, civil war, as in Nigeria (1967–70). With most avenues for peaceful protest closed, the political opposition or excluded regions/groups in some countries took to armed violence in their struggles for power or freedom (Ake 1996: 6; Ayittey 1992).

Thus, between 1963 and 1990, there were some 38 actual and attempted *coups* in the sub-region, even as several states remained under authoritarian one-party regimes. Although the coups were undertaken by the military, often segments of the civilian population sympathetic to the ideals of the coup leaders were armed and entrusted with the duty of enforcing the precepts of the military regimes. In some cases, trade unionists, students and unemployed youth at the periphery of society were given arms and constituted as civil defence forces with the mandate to police their societies and bring to book violators of the new and often radical code of the coup leaders. Such coups, therefore, "exarcebated the diffusion of arms into the civilian domain" (Musah 2002: 917). It must, however, be noted that the proliferation of arms during this period was not on such a wide scale on account of several challenges, including transportation and obtaining funds for payment. These two challenges have fallen away, as globalisation has provided options for transportation and globalised finance allows for easy transactions throughout the world – even in illicit goods.

The governance challenges discussed above reached a climax late in the 1980s, resulting in armed conflicts in several countries in the sub-region. Liberia and Sierra Leone became the examples of "failed states" in West Africa on account of the brutal civil wars that ravaged them (and threatened neighbouring states), but there were also small-scale insurgencies in Guinea, Senegal and Mali. These conflicts were fuelled and sustained by a guaranteed supply of SALW made more readily available in the countries of Europe freed from the control of the former Soviet Union (Stevenson 2005). However, even though these arms were meant for rebel and dissident groups, there were instances of covert assistance from states within and outside the sub-region. There is ample evidence in the reports of the United Nations expert panels on Liberia and Sierra Leone demonstrating the collusion between criminal weapons dealers and neighbouring states in supplying weapons to rebel groups, even where Security Council arms embargoes were in place.

These UN reports point us in two useful directions. Judging from the modes of transportation outlined in the reports, there was clear and direct involvement of governments in supplying weapons to state and non-state actors in violation of UN embargoes. Second, there is what appears to be exploitation of the lack of due diligence on the part of other states in the enforcement of the arms control bans.[1] Despite the lack of clarity, both scenarios are useful for our discussions because they form part of the supply chain of arms into the sub-region.

The evidence in the report of the UN panel of experts on Liberia (UNSC 2001) shows that diversions also occurred on the "blind side" of authorities. In the report, the experts indicated that weapons meant for Uganda were diverted to Liberia after Uganda rejected the consignment as not meeting the contractual requirements. Upon this rejection, the broker was requested to send the consignment back to the country of origin, Slovakia. However, instead, "the Egyptian arms broker sold them to a company in Guinea that turned out to be a front for a Liberian smuggling network" (UNSC 2001: 11). The first consignment was supplied without problem to the new buyer, but the Ugandan government impounded the second consignment. Clearly, the Ugandan government had not known about the first diversion, which was taking place on the blind side of the authorities.

Illicit proliferations are also often piggy-backed on licit sources. This means that illicit purchases and transfers are done through the alteration and falsification of geniune end-user certificates, insurance and other forms of documenta-

---

1. It is unclear whether the governments and/officials of Benin, Côte d'ivoire, Nigeria and Togo were aware that the Antonov 12 to which they had granted rights to their air space (and which later crashed in Liberia on 15 February 2002) was transporting arms.

tion and flight diversions either in collusion with governments or without their knowledge (UNSC 2001; Griffiths and Wilkinson 2007).

According to the UN reports, it was apparent that an illicit arms cartel was using forged duplicates of end-user certificates from countries such as Guinea. Given the frequency with which forged end-user certificates have been traced to Guinea, it is difficult to imagine that Guinea's officials were unaware that certificates issued by them were being modified by others. As mentioned above, the danger for West Africa is that once SALWs enter the sub-region, it is easy for them to be diffused because of the porous borders and weak security mechanisms for identification, detection and confiscation.

Another source of proliferation is the SALWs designated for peacekeeping and peace support operations. Such weapons may fall into the wrong hands when rebel groups kidnap peacekeepers. Eric Berman (2001) provides a catalogue of incidents during which arms were seized from peacekeepers. For instance, according to Berman, the RUF captured a considerable amount of weapons and ammunition from peacekeepers during the battle for Freetown and also "routed ECOMOG [ECOWAS's monitoring group] at Kono where the West African force had stationed most of its materiel, capturing all its weapons, including three tanks" (Berman 2001: 9). The RUF also captured weapons by ambushing peacekeepers. In 2000, RUF captured 500 United Nations peacekeepers. Although they were freed and some heavy military weapons were returned (Leighton 2000), most probably because the rebels feared that their size made them easily visible, there were no reports of other weapons and equipment being returned. It can be safely concluded that the peacekeepers' small arms (probably on account of their small size) were among the weapons and equipment not returned (Leighton 2000).

Berman (2001: 10) notes that when members of the Kenyan contingent were captured by the RUF in January 2000, it is believed that they took "eight G-3 rifles, one pistol and several hundred rounds of small arms ammunition". Again, when the Zambian contingent was captured, he surmises the RUF took about "500 AK-47 rifles, a few dozen machine guns, assorted mortars, and several tons of small arms ammunition" (Berman 2001: 10). The Kenyan contingent is also understood to have lost a considerable amount of materiel to the RUF when it was taken hostage. A company of Nigerian soldiers was relieved of their weapons after being ambushed by the RUF in April 2000, whilst a detachment of 21 Indian officers was also disarmed after being detained by the RUF in May. The numbers presented here relate to the RUF. This means that other groups may also have obtained weapons using similar tactics: the West Side Boys, for instance, also captured peacekeepers during the conflict.

Peacekeepers are also alleged to have sold their weapons while on peace support missions in exchange for various commodities. Berman (2001: 9) suggests that ECOMOG troops sold weapons in exchange for "cash, diamonds, food and medicine". He questions the supposed loss of the Guinean troops' equipment and weapons on 10 January 2000, and notes that Western diplomats, the UN and the Mission in Sierra Leone agreed there had been some underhand dealing in the "capture". In the Democratic Republic of the Congo, UN peacekeepers were accused of trading their guns for gold (Plaut 2007).

Although the UN has dismissed these allegations about its peacekeepers in the Congo, the organisation has been accused of trying to cover up. Testifying in his defence, former Liberian President Charles Taylor confessed he had purchased arms from Nigerian ECOMOG peacekeepers in Liberia during the civil war (Sesay 2009). If these assertions are true, they again suggest that peacekeeping/peace support operations can contribute to the proliferation of weapons in the sub-region.

Disarmament programmes at the end of the conflicts in Sierra Leone and Liberia were unable to mop up all the SALW, especially since some of them had found their way into other theatres of conflict in the sub-region. Consequently, although SALW are not new to West Africa, their current number – seven million are reportedly in circulation – is unprecedented in the history of the sub-region (Small Arms Survey 2001:63). Available evidence indicates arms sales by ex-combatants to other groups in the sub-region engaged in armed struggles (Duquet 2009: 178).

At the end of their tour of duty, some returning security and peacekeeping officers are able to smuggle in weapons either bought for paltry sums or taken as spoils from killed or captured combatants.

Another source of arms into the sub-region has been through the private military companies (PMCs) providing security in troubled countries. The Sandline affair illustrates the dilemma of utilising PMCs in the face of the failure of the international community to act decisively. In 1997, after the overthrow of Sierra Leonean President Ahmed Tejan Kabbah, arrangements were made with Sandline International for the provision of military equipment and services. Despite a Security Council arms embargo, the Sierra Leonean government provided an end-user certificate for the procurement and transportation of arms into Sierra Leone. The "Report of the Sierra Leone Arms Investigation" by Sir Thomas Legg and Sir Robin Ibbs suggests that this was a violation of the arms embargo because of ignorance on the part of those who should have known, such as Peter Penfold and President Kabbah (Legg and Ibbs 1998). For the purposes of this discussion, the Sandline affair illustrates the possibilities of circumventing arms embargoes by using the services of PMCs, whose legality is shrouded in complexity.

Government arms stockpiles can also be sources of illicit proliferation. Duquet (2009), using Nigeria's Niger Delta as a case study, argues that this was the case at the outset of the insurgency when rebel groups had not yet fully tapped into the oil "war economy". It is, however, noteworthy that proliferation from government stockpiles can also take place in the absence of armed conflict, for instance during prison breaks and/or break-ins by criminal groups in need of weapons. State security forces are also identified as a source of illicit small arms proliferation. Although Nigeria is referred to in Duquet's work, the phenomenon is by no means limited to Nigeria. For example, on 17 May 2008, Ghanaian police reported the arrest of one of its officers for attempting to sell an AK-47 and 30 rounds of ammunition to a member of a warring faction in a conflict that had necessitated deployment of a contigent of police to provide security. The arrested officer was a member of this police contigent.

Arms collected during disarmament and demobilisation and diverted for sale on the black market by unscrupulous/rogue officers may also be a source of SALW proliferation. It must be noted, however, that the lack of data on the pilfering of arms from official stockspiles makes it challenging to ascertain the numbers involved and more research is needed to generate the data required for assessment.

Duquet (2009) raises concerns about maritime security in the area adjoining Nigeria's restive oil-rich Niger Delta region. According to him, the Niger Delta's proximity to international waters facilitates smuggling and piracy in the waters of the Gulf of Guinea. Duquet pinpoints a critical component in illicit arms proliferation – the effective organisation of and resources available to organised criminal networks. He states that smugglers from Guinea-Bissau, Gabon and Cameroon, using speedboats, purchase weapons from vessels on the high seas for sale to groups in the Niger Delta (Duquet 2009: 177).

With the exception of Guinea-Bissau, the two other countries are not members of ECOWAS and hence party to its convention. Yet, the inter-regional transportation of arms is relatively easy once the arms are in the sub-region. The lack of systematic research into marine (in)security and its contribution to small arms proliferation makes it difficult to reach general conclusions on the phenomenon in the sub-region. However, the example of the Niger Delta suggests that there could be similar instances in other coastal countries.

As mentioned earlier, the porous borders in the sub-region allow for easy transportation of arms using the same routes and methods employed for smuggling other goods from one country to another. Arms from conflict zones may be transported through the so-called ant-trade: smuggling a few at a time along with other contraband goods using illegal routes or hidden in legal cargo being transported across borders. On 3 March 2011, a federal judge sentenced a self-confessed arms trafficker to serve a jail term in the United States for concealing weapons in containers used for the shipment of vehicles to Nigeria (Associated Press 2011). In a similar development, operatives of the Nigerian State Security Service on 27 October 2010 intercepted a considerable number of rocket launchers, grenades and other explosives hidden under tiles in 13 containers (BBC 2010). Further research is, however, needed to ascertain the pervasiveness of this source of proliferation within the sub-region.

Local or craft manufacture by blacksmiths in the sub-region may also give rise to proliferation. Studies show that local blacksmiths have in response to the downturn in agriculture and crop prices, shifted to the manufacture of craft guns as a survival strategy and means of earning higher incomes. Countries such as Mali and Nigeria allow the manufacture of some types of small arms in local defence industries for use by their military and defence sectors,[2] but such manufacture is illegal in several other countries in the sub-region. A number of challenges arise in relation to local manufacture. There is a lack of consistently reliable data on the types and quantities of weapons produced and there are violations of production licences as manufacturers engage in the production of non-authorised weapons.[3] In addition, producers often operate with old licences, which makes it difficult to estimate how many producers exist and the number of weapons manufactured. Apart from this, underground industries exist in countries where local production is illegal and criminalised. Aning (2005), writing on Ghana where there is a ban on gun production, suggests that there are about 2,500 blacksmiths with the capacity to produce guns in two of Ghana's 10 regions, Ashanti and Brong Ahafo, and estimates annual production of some 200,000 firearms. The denial by states of the existence of the problem makes it difficult to devise appropriate responses.

Demand and Supply of SALW in West Africa

Arms control efforts must be take good account of the rationale for the demand and supply of arms. Demand drives supply and so arms proliferate because they serve a purpose, respond to identified needs and yield profits. Efforts to control small arms proliferation must therefore address the demand side as rigorously as the supply side. Small arms are procured because they are a means to an end, whether that be the non-threatening enhancement of status; sport and hunting; defensive functions by the state and individuals; or offensive use by criminal

---

2. The Defence Industries Corporation of Nigeria (DICON) produces limited supplies of small arms and ammunition for the army and security sector.
3. This point was explained to me by security officials from Mali and Burkina Faso during a training course on the marking and tracing of small arms at the Kofi Anan International Peacekeeping Training Centre, Accra. Their identities are protected because they were at the course as nominees of their institutions and were not authorised to grant interviews.

elements. Demands are generated where there are available means to meet a need. Brauer and Muggah suggest that demand "is a function of motivations and means" (2006: 139).

Although small arms are considered cheap, that assumption is relative, especially in West Africa, where the majority of persons live on less than $2 a day. In this context, small arms cannot be considered cheap. In 2005, the price of a locally manufactured single-barrel gun in Ghana was between $100-$200 (Aning 2005). Imported guns, depending on type, are even more expensive, ranging between $570 and $2,150 in the Niger Delta (Florquin and Berman 2005: 342).

Guns have acquired a currency of their own though and can be bartered for other items. However, ultimately, there must be the means – in cash or kind – to procure, otherwise there would be little demand. Limited access through the reduction of physical availability and/or stringent requirements for acquisition would induce scarcity, increase prices and reduce demand. Consequently, small arms control must simultaneously address the reasons that give rise to the need as well as the physical access.

According to the West African Action Network on Small Arms (WAANSA 2009) "the proliferation and misuse of small arms continue to threaten the security of people and nations in West Africa". Reliable estimates are difficult to come by, but according to one, about "eight to ten million illicit weapons are concentrated in West Africa" (Bah 2004: 33). What is, however, clear is that the scope of the threat posed by SALW proliferation is such that law enforcement agencies are in some instances overwhelmed by the activities of criminal gangs (Everts 2003:1 53).

Information available from public sources suggests an increase in the numbers of crimes as well as their viciousness. There are also more brazen attacks, such as daylight armed robberies, which were absent in certain countries. Anecdotal evidence suggests an increase in the acquisition of firearms by citizens who are unsure of the ability of law enforcement agencies to protect them. Small arms are the preferred weapons of choice among criminals because of their durability and portability (UNDP 2005).

What is, however, unclear is whether criminals demand weapons because they are interested in acquiring and possessing them or merely interested in obtaining access to them for specific periods. If the former, demand for the weapons themselves could be high, driving the supply side. However, if the latter, it is much more likely that criminals may consider sharing weapons among themselves and rather demand ammunition for the weapons. In this case, efforts at controlling ammunition must be enhanced to minimise its availability.

More attention needs to be paid to the ways in which some non-state actors come by SALWs. Coulibaly (2008: 6) makes the point that proliferation can be by "legal means". It is also noted that during conflict some West African states have liberalised gun possession laws "to stimulate civilian arming. Arms were directly distributed to paramilitary groups by governments in order to fight rebel forces during the civil wars in Côte d'Ivoire, Liberia and Sierra Leone, but legislation was also liberalized, and proved a major driver of small arms diffusion".

It is also not unusual for political elites to arm local militias or unemployed youth for political ends, as occurred during the 2007 elections in Nigeria, when armed gangs were used to terrorise political opponents. Similarly, armed gangs are used to settle scores in intra-communal or sectarian conflict. More often than not, elite patrons abandon these gangs after they serve their purpose, leaving them to turn their arms over to opportunistic criminal enterprises.

Several countries in the sub-region are experiencing low-intensity armed conflicts involving state and non-state actors. In Nigeria, militants in the Niger Delta constantly battle with state security forces; in Ghana, there are latent conflicts mainly in the northern region which sometimes erupt into armed violence; and there are occasional skirmishes in the Casamance region of Senegal. Those engaged in these violent conflicts require arms. Attempts to address the proliferation of small arms and ammunition in the sub-region must therefore unpack the motivation and demand elements so that appropriate interventions for the regulation, detection and confiscation of illicit weapons can be designed.

ECOWAS and SALW Proliferation: From Moratorium to Convention

In the face of overwhelming evidence of a massive in-flow of SALWs into and within the sub-region and its likely effects on violent conflict and cross-border crime, serious efforts to control SALW in West Africa gathered momentum in the mid-1990s. The recognition that the small arms menace could not be dealt with singlehandedly by any individual state informed the decision of the then president of Mali, Alpha Konaré, to propose to ECOWAS leaders a moratorium on small arms transfers into the sub-region.

This followed a successful trial moratorium on SALW in Mali, where there had been a seemingly intractable conflict between the Tuaregs in the north of the country and the Malian government. His proposal was accepted by most governments and on 31 October 1989 a Moratorium on the Importation, Exportation and Manufacture of Light Weapons was signed in Abuja for an initial period of three years. It was extended at the end of the period for another three-year period, making it valid until 31 October 2004. The adoption of the moratorium was followed by the adoption of a code of conduct for its implementation in 1999. The moratorium was the first of its kind in Africa (Coulibaly 2008: 1), and it quickly gained the support of UNDP through the Programme for Coordination and Assistance for Security and Development (PCASED) in

1999. However, the moratorium had little impact on SALW proliferation, which continued to be writ large in the brutal civil wars that ravaged the Mano River Union (MRU) countries in the 1990s.[4]

It was noted that the "effectiveness of the Moratorium was impaired by its voluntary nature and the lack of enforceable sanctions" (Coulibaly 2008: 2). This situation led some groups within civil society to advocate a more comprehensive and effective protocol when the moratorium came up for renewal in 2004. These civil society groups organised as the West African Action Network on Small Arms (WAANSA), and with support from other civil society organisations and the international community (notably the International Action Network on Small Arms – IANSA – Oxfam and Amnesty International) played a central role in advocating stricter regional mechanisms for regulating SALW flows, in line with the global discourse on the ATT (Coulibaly 2008: Ibid).

These efforts, coupled with the changed context brought about by the 1993 revised ECOWAS treaty, contributed to the decision by ECOWAS leaders to take a more coordinated stand against the illegal trade in small arms. This led to the promulgation of a legally binding ECOWAS Convention on Small Arms and Light Weapons, their Ammunition and Other Related Materials in 2006 to regulate the proliferation of SALW in the sub-region.[5] This was an important step by West African leaders to enhance regional security. Its ratification and subsequent entry into force in 2009 followed the depositing of the ninth instrument of ratification by Benin. Ratification of the convention underscored the recognition of the nexus between arms proliferation, violence and crime, and marked a significant milestone in regional efforts in Africa to curb the menace of SALW proliferation and its threat to peace and development.

With the adoption of the convention in 2006, the ECOWAS Small Arms Control Programme (ECOSAP) was established "to build the capacities of the 15 ECOWAS member states [Benin, Burkina-Faso, Cape Verde, Côte d'Ivoire, Gambia, Ghana, Guinea, Guinea-Bissau, Liberia, Mali, Niger, Nigeria, Senegal, Sierra Leone and Togo] in combating the proliferation and illicit circulation of small arms in West Africa" (ECOSAP webpage). Since its inception, ECOSAP has facilitated the establishment of National Commissions of Small Arms and Light Weapons Control (NATCOM), provided them support in terms of capacity building and resources and coordinated their activities at the regional level,

---

4. The MRU countries are Liberia, Sierra Leone and Guinea.
5. ECOWAS convention defines light weapons as "Portable Arms designed to be used by several persons working together in a team"; small arms as "Arms used by one person"; ammunition as "Devices destined to be shot or projected through the means of firearms", and other related materials as "All components, parts or spare parts for small arms or light weapons or ammunition necessary for their functioning; or any chemical substance serving as active material used as propelling or explosive agent" (ECOWAS Convention 2006: 8–9).

including linkages with international partners and processes. ECOSAP has continued to partner with WAANSA and other national-level civil society organisations (ECOSAP Annual Report 2010). ECOSAP is supported by international donors: UNDP, EU, Spain, Sweden, France, Japan, Norway, Finland and the Netherlands (ECOSAP webpage).

Since the convention came into force, the major challenge has been ensuring full compliance by the governments of ECOWAS member states regarding its full implementation. The success of the convention has remained highly dependent on the development of robust mechanisms, the training of qualified personnel and the institution of relevant national structures to fight proliferation. It is, therefore, important to further examine the provisions of the convention.

Insights into the ECOWAS Convention on SALW

The ECOWAS convention is innovative. It is also pragmatic, and does not place a categorical ban on SALW, being aware of different national regimes and the impossibility of enforcing utopian ideals of arms control. Though focused, the convention is flexible enough to allow for small arms acquisition, possession and use, on condition that West African governments guarantee regulation and control within their territories. It also addresses small arms, light weapons and ammunition. The inclusion of the latter is particularly important, because although arms have a long lifespan, they are only useful with ammunition. Although there has been enhanced international cooperation in addressing the illicit proliferation of small arms, efforts at controlling the proliferation of ammunition are still limited (Herron *et al.* 2010).

The addition of ammunition and other related material, the definition of tracing and the inclusion of non-state actors as subjects of the convention as well as partners in the anti-trafficking efforts are among the convention's innovative and pragmatic provisions. They show that the convention draws substantially on the lessons learnt in the sub-region by placing a ban on the transfer of SALW and their manufacturing materials into the sub-region under Article 3 (1).

Furthermore, by enshrining provisions to cut off the source of materials for repairs and prohibiting the transfer of arms from and through member-state territories, the convention places an obligation on member states to ensure that SALW are not transported through their sea, land and air space into other territories. Article 3(3) unambiguously states that SALW are not goods as stipulated under the revised ECOWAS treaty, while Article 3(2) categorically bans the transfer of arms to non-state actors except with the express authorisation of the state into which imports are being made.

However, in recognition of legitimate defence needs, there are caveats for exemptions, and states can apply for exemption certificates to procure weapons for their national security, defence and law enforcement use, or for regional peacekeeping missions, evidence of which must be provided for assessment by the ECOWAS Commission. Conditions for exemptions are set out in Article 4. One of these conditions is that states have to establish and maintain an effective system for authorising the import and export of SALW, including for transit and transfer purposes.

Article 5 of the convention sets out the detailed requirements for an exemption request, including the quantity, exact types duly marked under the ECOWAS classification system, supplier details, number and period of shipments as well as transportation type, transit locations, end user and the end use to which the arms will be put. The ECOWAS president (formerly the executive secretary) evaluates the information submitted and responds confidentially to the requesting state. The final decision on granting an exemption certificate is taken by consensus of ECOWAS member states. However, in cases where member-states can't reach a consensus, the opinion of the president earlier transmitted to the requesting country and the exemption request form "shall be transmitted to the Mediation and Security Council of ECOWAS for a final decision".

Once issued, the exemption certificate must accompany requests for export licences. This is an essential tool in addressing the challenge of diversions, excessive stockpiling and the abuse of end-user certificates. The utility of the exemption certificate is enhanced by the fact that ECOWAS works in concert with other arms control regimes such as the Wassenaar Arrangement,[6] the EU through its dual use export controls and the OSCE's regime for combating illicit proliferation and trafficking in small arms. This collaboration provides a wide geographical scope within which the exemption certificate is relevant.

The exemption certificate also addresses the challenge posed by rogue governments who in the past supported illicit proliferation by providing criminal non-state actors with end-user certificates. As a further measure of transparency, the president of the Commission is required to publish a comprehensive annual list detailing all the exemptions granted and refused. The exemption certificate is valid for one year (ECOWAS 2010).

The third chapter of the convention provides minimum standards for the regulation of small arms manufacture within states. States are charged with the responsibility of evolving national mechanisms within the framework of

---

6. The following states are party to the agreement: Argentina, Australia, Austria, Belgium, Bulgaria, Canada, Croatia, Czech Republic, Denmark, Estonia, Finland, France, Germany, Greece, Hungary, Ireland, Italy, Japan, Latvia, Lithuania, Luxembourg, Malta, Netherlands, New Zealand, Norway, Poland, Portugal, Republic of Korea, Romania, Russian Federation, Slovakia, Slovenia, South Africa, Spain, Sweden, Switzerland, Turkey, Ukraine, United Kingdom and United States.

the convention for addressing local manufacture in their territories. The framers of the convention failed to get into the debate on whether SALW manufacture should be criminalised, leaving this thorny issue to individual national legislatures to regulate. States are, nonetheless, required to furnish the ECOWAS president with complete information on the extant manufacturers within their territories, their production capacity, the types of arms manufactured and their annual output, which must be recorded in the national registries.

Article 8 provides two conditions to guide states in authorising manufacture. Manufacturers must provide the quantity, exact types and kinds of arms using the ECOWAS classification system, including all serial numbers and other markings as well as the procedure for marking and entering records of production into the national registry. The requesting entity also has to provide information on post-production storage and management of weapons. Without this information, authorisation for manufacture should not be given. In addition, Article 9 provides requirements to enhance transparency and promote confidence and trust among states. Article 9(1) obliges state parties to establish computerised databases for keeping records of SALW. The computerisation of the records relates to the requirement in Article 9(3) that member states keep the records in the databases permanently.

Article 9(2) (e) is an effort to control illicit proliferation by following the money trail. It requires documentation of the insurers and financial institution(s) involved in the supply process. This requirement allows for engagement between states and financial institutions in the fight against the proliferation of small arms in the sub-region.

Article 12 provides a framework for dialogue between the ECOWAS Commission, member states and manufacturers and suppliers as well as other international and regional organisations involved in anti-proliferation efforts. These provisions promote confidence among legal manufacturers, suppliers and states and acknowledge that small arms production is first and foremost a legitimate commercial venture, which, like other commercial ventures, needs to be safeguarded against criminal elements. Gaining buy-in among legal manufacturers and suppliers for the convention facilitates vigilance on their part and guarantees that attention is paid to the supply and distribution networks.

States are also obliged to develop measures and standards for the effective management of government and private arms stockpiles. This is to guarantee the safety of citizens as well as the security of the arms. Mismanagement of stockpiles can result in lethal accidents. Again, mismanaged stocks facilitate pilfering and the seepage of licit stocks on to the illicit market. States are also to develop mechanisms for monitoring compliance with established standards.

To effectively keep track of small arms, light weapons and ammunition, the convention specifies that each be duly marked in a particular way. Markings are the "DNA" of SALW. They contain "genetic" information of SALW such as the manufacturer, country or place of manufacture, serial number(s) and any other unique user markings with a numeric/alphanumeric code for easy identification by all states. Article 18 insists on particular types of markings on weapons allowed within the sub-region.

Chapter 6 of the convention provides for institutional and implementation arrangements. It identifies actors and mechanisms for implementing and evaluating the convention and assigns responsibility for the performance of certain roles. Some of these actions are directly ascribed to member states: the establishment of NATCOMs and development of plans of action; strengthening capacity of national security forces; sub-regional cooperation; and partnership with civil society. At the sub-regional level, the president of the ECOWAS Commission can appoint a group of independent experts to support him in monitoring and evaluating implementation of the convention. These experts, who will have access to all relevant information, will submit a yearly report to the president.

As already mentioned, involvement of private entities in the arms trade requires the permission of states, which are obliged to register all brokering entities incorporated within their territories. The convention stipulates that registered brokers obtain explicit authorisation for all individual transactions in which they are involved irrespective of the place of transaction. To avoid diversions, states are to demand that brokers fully disclose all documentation, including import and export licences, transaction details, all brokers and shipping agents involved as well as transportation details, including place of origin, transit and destination. States are to develop legislative measures to criminalise and penalise illicit brokering within their territories.

The convention calls for harmonisation of relevant legislative principles within states as well as collaboration between states to facilitate smooth implementation of the convention. Capacity development for state security institutions and personnel is imperative to combat illicit proliferation, which may operate on its own or be part of a network of organised criminal activities.

The ECOWAS Commission is assigned a significant role in implementing the convention. States are also encouraged to promote intra-agency and interstate collaboration to enhance the opportunities for realising the ideals of the convention. Article 25 provides a non-exhaustive list of actions to be undertaken by the Commission. These include providing technical and financial assistance for the implementation of the convention; guaranteeing a systematic and systemic approach to the development of structures to implement the convention; and developing an action plan for the convention.

In recognition of the need for a multi-sectoral approach to control efforts, the convention allocates specific responsibility to different sectors of the state. Legislatures in the sub-region are charged with developing the right legal instruments for the control efforts. They are therefore requested in Article 21 to revise their national legislation to ensure conformity with the principles of the convention as well as to criminalise circumvention of the convention and United Nations arms embargoes. In addition, national legislatures are required to harmonise their legislation to encourage uniform control standards in the sub-region. For law enforcement and security sectors to be able to cooperate effectively within their countries as well as with others in the sub-region, it is important to have the right policy and legal frameworks, which must be provided for by the legislature. Harmonisation of legislation is therefore also useful in facilitating collaboration among law enforcement and security agencies in the sub-region.

There is no gainsaying that the success of the ECOWAS convention is highly dependent on effective cooperation among member states in the sub-region. The porosity of borders in West Africa means that it is possible for criminals, mercenaries, armed fighters and SALW traders to outwit poorly resourced security agencies by moving between various countries in the sub-region.

It should be noted that the fight against illicit SALW proliferation cannot be won by state security institutions alone (even though they are critical). The pervasiveness of the challenge giving rise to the demand and supply of SALW makes bringing the public on board in the control efforts imperative. Aware of the general lack of knowledge of Community citizens about the laws and rules of the Community, the drafters of the convention obligated states in Article 23 to design appropriate programmes for community education and awareness. The convention needs to be popularised so that citizens become more aware of (a) the challenges of SALW, especially through a public health lens; (b) the rules governing acquisition, possession and use of SALW within the sub-region and, most importantly, within their countries of origin and residence; and (c) the criminal nature of illicit proliferation, acquisition, possession and use. This strategy could be useful in eliciting information on illegal manufacturers, suppliers and individual ownership.

Member states are further requested in Article 23(3) to encourage civil society organisations to play leading roles in publicising the convention. In addition, civil society movements usually have budgets for such activities and also the resources to raise the needed funds for such activities even when there are budgetary constraints. Thus, this provision will be useful in ensuring that the provisions of the convention are widely disseminated within states.

Article 27 spells out the procedure for making complaints in the event of a breach of the convention. The procedure is available to both states and individuals. A complaint may be brought to the attention of the ECOWAS president, who can submit it to the ECOWAS Mediation and Security Council, which decides on the veracity of a claim and on an appropriate response where violation is established. The powers available to the Mediation and Security Council are spelt out in Article 27(2) and include sanctions, inquiry, study or a referral to the ECOWAS Court of Justice. A state or individual may also refer a perceived breach of the convention directly to the ECOWAS Court of Justice.

The convention also has an inbuilt mechanism for monitoring compliance by states. In terms of Article 28 the president of the Commission can appoints a group of independent experts to support him in monitoring compliance. The GIEs are required to monitor exemption requests and submit reports to the president of the Commission.

However, in spite of its innovative provisions and sophistication, the ECOWAS SALW convention still faces considerable challenges in terms of the capacity of the relevant national and regional institutions, the political will of member states, resource deficits and the sophistication of and ample resources available to transnational criminal networks operating in the sub-region.

Implementing the ECOWAS SALW Convention: The Challenges

Due to the existence of the UNPoA as well as the Firearms Protocol, a number of building blocks had already been laid for the implementation of the convention. Thus, some progress has been made in implementing it. With the exception of Gambia, Guinea, Guinea-Bissau and Côte d'Ivoire, all members of ECOWAS are parties to the convention. Thirteen of the 15 members of ECOWAS have also established NATCOMs, the co-ordinating framework for addressing small arms, light weapons, ammunition and related materials issues. Although one of the fundamental challenges of small arms control has been the lack of institutional capacity (ECOSAP Annual Report 2010), efforts continue to train security sector personnel and law enforcement agencies on the mechanisms for addressing small arms proliferation.

However, there is a dearth of technological equipment needed to combat such proliferation in the sub-region. For instance, metal detectors are either absent or woefully inadequate at points of entry into several countries. Several airports as well as seaports in the sub-region lack scanners, which are essential for the detection of contraband goods, including weapons concealed in luggage. The shortage of equipment is compounded by the lack of spare parts, supporting infrastructure and the dependency on external sources of supply.

Despite the nexus between small arms and other transnational crimes, small arms control has not received the attention shown by the international community towards the illegal drug/narcotics trade. This has meant that while border posts in the sub-region have benefited from state-of-the-art drug detection equipment, the same cannot be said for small arms control efforts. The evidence for illicit proliferation suggests that air transportation is the preferred means for inter-continental transfers of arms by criminal networks (Griffiths 2007). However, arms are also trafficked by sea (Keili 2008). Once the arms reach a country within the sub-region, transporting them within and between countries is relatively easy, due in part to the sub-region's porous borders and weak law-enforcement mechanisms.

The lack of the appropriate equipment at land and sea ports has meant that law enforcement officers face difficulties in identifying and confiscating illicit weapons. Immigration and customs officials at land borders lack the technology to scan cargoes for the detection of arms, making it challenging to address inter- and intra-country transfers by land. Given that large trucks laden with goods criss-cross several countries in the sub-region, it is impractical to expect border personnel to offload each vehicle for inspection.[7] Implementing Article 22 of the convention, which aims at strengthening border controls, is a major prerequisite for detecting and confiscating new entries into the sub-region and in achieving the objectives of the convention.

Apart from the paucity of large cargo scanners, there is also the scarcity of resources for record keeping. Article 9 of the convention stipulates that states establish computerised national databases for the purposes of record keeping. The databases are expected to be compiled using information from the various sectors responsible for small arms control. The challenge lies in the insufficient investment in information storage and retrieval systems. Computers are a useful first step in record keeping, but also requited are adequate storage and retrieval systems designed to protect records against power surges, power outages, fire, floods, cyber-attacks, etc. Unfortunately, the basic backup systems in several offices make it difficult to assure the security of data in the event of such occurrences.

There are also other challenges with computer facilities in some countries in the sub-region that put into question the safety and integrity of data. Where computers exist, there are questions about their effective use and maintenance. For instance, a request by this researcher to visit a registry in Ghana was declined because, according to the officials there, it was impossible to access the computers, whose cables had been destroyed by rats. While this excuse appears ludicrous, it did raise fundamental questions about the supervisory mechanisms within states to ensure that databases are protected sufficiently.

ECOSAP has provided financial assistance to several NATCOMs to enable them to renovate and equip their offices, and even pays members of staff (ECOSAP Annual Report 2010). Although such activities fall within ECOSAP's mandate, care must be taken to ensure that member states do not shift their re-

---

7. I am grateful to the Malian and Burkinabe customs officials who shared this information with me during a training session at the Kofi Anan International Peacekeeping Training Centre.

sponsibilities on to the programme, particularly as ECOSAP is heavily dependent on donor assistance and funding. Although this funding is predictable in the short-to-medium term, it is important to minimise dependency on external sources as such assistance raises questions about autonomy and sustainability.

It is also noteworthy that most ECOWAS member states face major socioeconomic challenges that impair their capacity to act both nationally and regionally. In spite of the best intentions of the convention, well-resourced transnational crime networks, corruption and bureaucratic politics within law enforcement agencies and high levels of poverty and youth unemployment in the sub-region, particularly in post-conflict societies, continue to undermine efforts to curb SALW proliferation. These factors explain why certain criminal and corrupt elements are able to exploit every opportunity, gap and weakness in the arms control mechanism and process.

Sub-regional efforts cannot be separated from the capacity and will of ECOWAS member states to act and coordinate their efforts with those at the regional and global levels. In this regard, optimal results from the faithful implementation of the convention will ultimately lie in the capacity of West African states to overcome their developmental challenges and institutional weaknesses and better coordinate their efforts at SALW regulation with relevant international mechanisms in a rapidly globalising and interdependent world.

Conclusion

The ECOWAS Convention on Small Arms and Light Weapons, their Ammunition and Other Related Materials is a progressive and innovative step in the fight against illicit arms proliferation in West Africa. It addresses several challenges to human and state security in the sub-region, including violence, cross-border drug and human trafficking, money laundering, smuggling and armed robberies, all linked to and sustained by SALW proliferation. In addition, the various insurrections and large-scale armed violence in the countries of the sub-region are also fuelled and sustained by easy access to SALW. Effective implementation of the convention will go a long way towards enhancing physical safety, socioeconomic security and political stability in West Africa.

Recommendations

A fundamental requirement for realising the convention's objectives is overcoming corruption and resolving problems linked to rather weak levels of accountability and participatory governance within ECOWAS member states.

Addressing corruption in law enforcement and security agencies means paying officials and operatives living wages and decent welfare packages and providing an enabling environment devoid of political interference within which they can practise the highest levels of professionalism. This should be complemented by providing state-of-the-art security and monitoring systems to facilitate efficiency and ensuring that officials comply with the high ethical standards required to ensure transparency and accountability. It is unfortunate that so much is expected of law enforcement officers and security personnel, who are among the worst-paid public officials in some West African countries.

Given the cost implications of the ECOWAS classification system, the sub-region may have to consider procuring marking equipment that could be used for meeting the additional marking requirements of the convention. According to Paoli (2010), the cost of entry-level laser marking machines is €30,000–35,000 or US$41,000–48,000, mechanical engraving machines €12,000–14,000 or US$16,000–19,000 and dot peen/micro-percussion machines €5,000–6,500 Euros or US$6,800–9,000. While such equipment may be too expensive for cash-strapped West African governments, it should be possible for ECOWAS working through ECOSAP to procure portable versions to provide a mobile marking service in the sub-region. This service could be undertaken at a lower cost to the state and to local manufacturers requiring the service.

It is suggested that quick-impact projects and alternative livelihood projects be devised (with local participation) and introduced into local communities engaged in manufacturing and selling craft guns as part of a trust- and confidence-building initiative, rather than resorting to wholesale criminalisation of entire communities. However, much care should be taken to ensure that initiatives designed to discourage local manufacture of small arms pay attention to the sustainability of the livelihood projects.

Although alternative livelihood projects cannot realistically match the revenue from illicit manufacture of small arms, such projects should yield reasonable returns and should involve participation by local people and stakeholders. Since blacksmiths and artisans are no longer limited to their home countries (Agbonton-Johnson, Adedeji and Marzal 2004), it would be rewarding if the alternative projects can be connected with ongoing integration efforts in the West African sub-region. There is some potential for this in the agricultural sector and in cottage industry, and a whole range of financial and macroeconomic instruments can be devised at the regional level to invest in local manufacturing of agro-processing and other technologies. These will go a long way to addressing issues of poverty reduction and unemployment, and provide incentives to move away from the local production of small arms.

As part of a larger body of legal norms and rules designed for building a peaceful and secure West Africa, the convention should be better harmonised and integrated with sub-regional instruments such as the revised ECOWAS treaty, the Protocol on the Mechanism for Conflict Prevention, Management, Resolution, Peacekeeping and Security and the Protocol on Democracy and Good Governance, all of which should be situated in the broader ECOWAS Conflict Prevention Framework (ECPF). All ECOWAS documents on conflict prevention and management are interrelated and interdependent and the success of one is dependent on the success of the other, hence the need for a holistic approach.

The challenge of transforming ECOWAS into a veritable tool for promoting peace, security and development ultimately rests with sub-regional leaders and political elites in member states, who should genuinely represent and prioritise the interests and basic needs of the citizens of their states. Related to this is the need for self-sufficiency and autonomy in resourcing ECOWAS's peace and security mechanisms and the capacity of its institutions. It would be difficult to address the existing challenges confronting the convention on SALW without a corresponding transformation of ECOWAS to reflect and prioritise the wishes of the peoples of the sub-region.

Another related issue is the reality of the conflict between national and regional interests, which undermines the ability of ECOWAS leaders to act on collective decisions. It is also not uncommon for some countries to go against decisions adopted at the summit level for no reason other than the personal interests of certain leaders or of their external strategic allies. This in more ways than one undermines collective efforts to implement mechanisms within the region's peace and security architecture.

Much attention has been given to the supportive role civil society has played, and plays in partnering with ECOSAP and various NATCOMs in West Africa. Even so, more attention should be focused on several aspects of civil society's role in promoting the regulation of SALWs in the sub-region. These relate to accountability and transparency within civil society itself, the institutional capacities and sustainability of these organisations, the interests they represent, and how they can better engage with and represent grassroots interests by building stronger connections between advocacy and participatory policy actions.

With specific reference to the convention, more emphasis should be placed on addressing the illicit proliferation of SALW, which persists as a formidable challenge to peace and security. Currently, there is no sub-regional system of blacklisting dealers in illicit SALWs. It would therefore be useful to develop such a system for identifying, blacklisting and sanctioning of those guilty of violating the provisions of the convention.

Although awareness of the harmful effects of SALW proliferation on conflict, insecurity, poverty and lack of sustained development in West Africa has grown, there is a need for more research of the kind that will produce knowledge that can lead to more informed policies for tackling SALW proliferation at its roots (rather than by focusing excessively on the symptoms). Of particular note is the need for more research into: the changing dynamics of arms proliferation in the sub-region and its connections with global and regional centres of production and distribution; factors that drive demand and supply; the evasion of effective monitoring, reporting and interdiction; a comparison of the impact of proliferation in different contexts; and the institutional and technological challenges and possible solutions in the form of actionable policies.

Bibliography

Aning, Emmanuel Kwesi, 2005, "The Anatomy of Ghana's Secret Arms Industry", in Florquin, Nicolas and Eric G. Berman (eds), *Armed and Aimless:Armed Groups, Guns, and Human Security in ECOWAS Region*. Geneva: Small Arms Survey, pp. 79-107.

Aning, Kwesi and Sarjoh A. Bah, 2010, *ECOWAS and Conflict Prevention in West Africa: Confronting the Triple Threats*. New York: New York University Center on International Cooperation.

Annan, Kofi A., 2000, *We the Peoples: The Role of the United Nations in the 21st Century*. New York: United Nations.

Associated Press, 2011, "The Breaking News Blog", *Washington Post*, 1 March, http://voices.washingtonpost.com (accessed 4 April 2011).

Bah, M.S., 2004, "Micro-Disarmament in West Africa: ECOWAS Moratorium on small arms and light weapons", *African Security Review* 13, 3.

Berman, Eric G., 2001, "Arming the Revolutionary United Front", *African Security Review* 10, 1.

Brauer, Jurgen and Robert Muggah, 2006, "Completing the Circle: Building a Theory of Small Arms Demand", *Contemporary Security Policy* 27, 1:138–54.

British Broadcasting Corporation, 2008a, "Mali cocaine haul after firefight", United Kingdom, 4 January.

—, 2008b, "S Leone police seize drugs plane", United Kingdom, 14 July.

—, 2010, "Nigeria's secret police intercept weapons shipment", 27 October, http://www.bbc.co.uk (accessed 27 October 2010).

—, 2011a, "Ivory Coast: French forces take over Abidjan Airport", London, 3 April.

—, 2011b, "Ivory Coast: Ouattara forces promise Abidjan offensive", 4 April, http://www.bbc.co.uk/news/world-africa-12953763 (accessed 4 April 2011).

Coulibaly, Mohamed, 2008, "From Moratorium to a Convention on small arms: A change in politics and practices for the 15 member countries of the Economic Community of West African States (ECOWAS)", in *From Poverty to Power: How Active Citizens and Effective States Can Change the World*. London: Oxfam International.

Duquet, Nils, 2009, "Arms Acquisition Patterns and the Dynamics of Armed Conflict: Lessons from the Niger Delta", *International Studies Perspectives* 10:169–85.

ECOWAS Commission, 2010, *Meeting of Ministers of Defence and Security to Review and Adopt the Plan of Action for the Implementation of ECOWAS Convention on Small Arms and Light Weapons and the Exemption Request Form to the Convention*. Meeting Report, Abuja: ECOWAS.

ECOWAS Convention on Small Arms and Light Weapons, Their Ammunition and Other Related Materials, 2006, http://www.iag-agi.org/bdf/docs/ecowas_convention_small_arms.pdf (accessed 16 September 2011)

ECOWAS Small Arms Control Programme (ECOSAP), 2010, Annual Report, http://www.ecosap.ecowas.int/index.php?option=com_jotloader&view=categories&cid=0_11910765ecb7da29da3ff7029b829ef0&Itemid=84&lang=en (accessed 16 September 2011).

Everts, Dan, 2003, "Human Trafficking: The Ruthless Trade in Human Misery", *Brown Journal of World Affairs* X, 1:149–58.

Florquin, Nicholas and Eric Berman (eds), 2005, *Armed and Aimless: Armed Groups, Guns, and Human Security in the ECOWAS Region*. Geneva: Small Arms Survey 2005.

Ghana News Agency, 2010, "INTERPOL arrests Johnson Kombian", *GhanaWeb*, 20 November, http://www.ghanaweb.com (accessed 25 April 2011).

GhanaWeb, 2011, "27 Delta militants arrested in Takoradi", *GhanaWeb*, 3 February, http://www.ghanaweb.com (accessed 28 April 2011).

Griffiths, Hugh and Adrian Wilkinson, 2007, *Guns, Planes and Ships Identification and Disruption of Clandestine Arms Transfer*. Belgrade: South Eastern and Eastern Europe Clearinghouse for the Control of Small Arms and Light Weapons.

Hazen, Jennifer M. and Jonas Horner, 2007, "Small Arms, Armed Violence, and Insecurity in Nigeria: The Niger Delta in Perspective", *Occassional Paper*. Geneva: Small Arms Survey, December.

Herron, Patrick, Jasna Lazarevic, Nic Marsh and Matt Schroeder, 2010, "Emerging from Obscurity: The Global Ammunition Trade", in Graduate Institute of International and Development Studies Small Arms Survey, *Small Arms Survey 2010: Gangs, Groups, and Guns*, Geneva: Cambridge University Press, pp. 7–39.

International Labour Organisation, 2007, *The Decent Work Agenda in Africa 2007–2015*. Report of the director-general. Geneva: International Labour Organisation.

—, 2011, *Report of the International Labour Office for the Fourth Conference on the Least Developed Countries*. Background conference report. Geneva: International Labour Organisation.

IRIN humanitarian news and analysis, May 2008, http://www.irinnews.org/IndepthMain.aspx?IndepthId=8&ReportId=58952 (accessed 15 September 2011)

Joyonline, 2011, "Ivorian paramilitary officers picked up by Ghana police", *Myjoyonline*, 1 April, http://news.myjoyonline.com (accessed 3 April 2011).

Keili, Francis, 2008, "Small arms and light weapons transfer in West Africa: A stocktaking", *Disarmament Forum: The Complex Dynamics of Small Arms in West Africa* no. 4. Geneva: United Nations Institute for Disarmament Research.

Knaup, Horand, 2010, "Hijacked Weapons: A Discreet Deal for the War in Sudan", *Spiegel Online International*, 12 September, http://www.spiegel.de/international/world (accessed 13 May 2011).

Legg, Thomas and Robin Ibbs, 1998, *Report of the Sierra Leone Arms Investigation*. London: House of Commons.

Leighton, Caspar, 2000, "New efforts to free hostages in S Leone after release of Five", *ReliefWeb*, 31 August, http://reliefweb.int (accessed 20 April 2011).

Migdal, Joel S., 1988, *Strong Societies and Weak States: State-Society Relations and State Capabilities in the Third World*. Princeton NJ: Princeton University Press.

Modern Ghana Group, 2007, "ModernGhana", 10 April, http://www.modernghana.com/news/133665/50/nkoranza-honours-amoateng.html (accessed 1 April 2011).

Musah, Abdel-Fatau, 2002, "Privatization of Security, Arms Proliferation and the Process of State Collapse", *Africa Development and Change* 33, 5:911–33.

Naylor, R.T., 2001, "The Rise of the Modern Arms Black Market and the Fall of Supply-Side Control", in Williams, Phil and Dimitri Vlassis (eds), *Combating Transnational Crime: Concepts, Activities and Responses*. Oxford: Frank Cass, pp. 209–36.

Obi, Cyril, 2009, "Economic Community of West African States on the Ground: Comparing Peacekeeping in Liberia, Sierra Leone, Ginea-Bissau and Coe d'Ivoire", *African Security* 2, 2–3.

Peace FM Online, 2011, *5 Chinese Galamseyers Nabbe*, Accra, 5 May.

Plaut, Martin, 2007, "UN troops 'traded gold for guns'", British Broadcasting Corporation, 23 May, http://news.bbc.co.uk/2/hi/6681457.stm (accessed 15 April 2011).

Prod. Ghana Web, 2008, *Policeman Arrested for attempted sale of AK 47*, Accra, 17 May.

Sesay, Alpha, 2009, "Taylor Negotiated With RUF Rebels For The Release Of UN Hostages; Says ECOMOG Traded Diamonds and Arms With the RUF". A Project of the Open Society Justice Initiative, 18 August, http://www.charlestaylortrial.org (accessed 12 April 2011).

Small Arms Survey, 2002, *Counting the human cost*. Oxford: Oxford University Press.

Stevenson, Jonathan, 2005, *The Flow of Small Arms and Explosives to Terrorist Groups*. Geneva: United Nations Institute for Disarmament Research.

United Nations Development Programme, 2005, *Securing Development: UNDP's support for addressing small arms issues*. New York: United Nations Development Programme.

United Nations Economic Commission for Africa, 2010, *Strategies to Promote Youth Self-employment in West Africa*. Meeting report. Dakar: United Nations Economic Commission for Africa.

United Nations Office on Drugs and Crime, 2010a, *Promoting Health, Security and Justice*. Annual report. Vienna: United Nations Office on Drugs and Crime.

—, 2010b, *World Drug Report 2010*. Annual report. Vienna: United Nations Office on Drugs and Crime.

United Nations Security Council, 2001, *Report of the Panel of Experts pursuant to Security Council resolution 1343 (2001), paragraph 19, concerning Liberia*. New York: United Nations.

—, 2002, *Report of the Panel of Experts appointed pursuant to Security Council resolution 1395 (2002), paragraph 4, in relation to Liberia*. New York: United Nations.

Wallacher, Hilde and Alexander Harang, 2011, *Small but Lethal: Small Arms Ammunitions and Arms Trade Treaty*. Oslo: PRIO.

West African Action Network on Small Arms (WAANSA), 2009, "BackGround Information: West African Action Network on Small Arms", http://www.waansa.org (accessed 2 April 2011).

Zartman, William I., 1995, *Collapsed States: The Disintegration and Restoration of Legitimate Authority.* Boulder CO: Lynne Rienner .

DISCUSSION PAPERS PUBLISHED BY THE INSTITUTE

Recent issues in the series are available electronically for download free of charge
www.nai.uu.se

1. Kenneth Hermele and Bertil Odén, *Sanctions and Dilemmas. Some Implications of Economic Sanctions against South Africa.*
   1988. 43 pp. ISBN 91-7106-286-6

2. Elling Njål Tjönneland, *Pax Pretoriana. The Fall of Apartheid and the Politics of Regional Destabilisation.*
   1989. 31 pp. ISBN 91-7106-292-0

3. Hans Gustafsson, Bertil Odén and Andreas Tegen, *South African Minerals. An Analysis of Western Dependence.*
   1990. 47 pp. ISBN 91-7106-307-2

4. Bertil Egerö, *South African Bantustans. From Dumping Grounds to Battlefronts.*
   1991. 46 pp. ISBN 91-7106-315-3

5. Carlos Lopes, *Enough is Enough! For an Alternative Diagnosis of the African Crisis.*
   1994. 38 pp. ISBN 91-7106-347-1

6. Annika Dahlberg, *Contesting Views and Changing Paradigms.*
   1994. 59 pp. ISBN 91-7106-357-9

7. Bertil Odén, *Southern African Futures. Critical Factors for Regional Development in Southern Africa.*
   1996. 35 pp. ISBN 91-7106-392-7

8. Colin Leys and Mahmood Mamdani, *Crisis and Reconstruction – African Perspectives.*
   1997. 26 pp. ISBN 91-7106-417-6

9. Gudrun Dahl, *Responsibility and Partnership in Swedish Aid Discourse.*
   2001. 30 pp. ISBN 91-7106-473-7

10. Henning Melber and Christopher Saunders, *Transition in Southern Africa – Comparative Aspects.*
    2001. 28 pp. ISBN 91-7106-480-X

11. *Regionalism and Regional Integration in Africa.*
    2001. 74 pp. ISBN 91-7106-484-2

12. Souleymane Bachir Diagne, et al., *Identity and Beyond: Rethinking Africanity.*
    2001. 33 pp. ISBN 91-7106-487-7

13. Georges Nzongola-Ntalaja, et al., *Africa in the New Millennium.* Edited by Raymond Suttner.
    2001. 53 pp. ISBN 91-7106-488-5

14. *Zimbabwe's Presidential Elections 2002.* Edited by Henning Melber.
    2002. 88 pp. ISBN 91-7106-490-7

15. Birgit Brock-Utne, *Language, Education and Democracy in Africa.*
    2002. 47 pp. ISBN 91-7106-491-5

16. Henning Melber et al., *The New Partnership for Africa's development (NEPAD).*
    2002. 36 pp. ISBN 91-7106-492-3

17. Juma Okuku, *Ethnicity, State Power and the Democratisation Process in Uganda.*
    2002. 42 pp. ISBN 91-7106-493-1

18. Yul Derek Davids, et al., *Measuring Democracy and Human Rights in Southern Africa.* Compiled by Henning Melber.
    2002. 50 pp. ISBN 91-7106-497-4

19. Michael Neocosmos, Raymond Suttner and Ian Taylor, *Political Cultures in Democratic South Africa.* Compiled by Henning Melber.
    2002. 52 pp. ISBN 91-7106-498-2

20. Martin Legassick, *Armed Struggle and Democracy. The Case of South Africa.*
    2002. 53 pp. ISBN 91-7106-504-0

21. Reinhart Kössler, Henning Melber and Per Strand, *Development from Below. A Namibian Case Study.*
    2003. 32 pp. ISBN 91-7106-507-5

22. Fred Hendricks, *Fault-Lines in South African Democracy. Continuing Crises of Inequality and Injustice.*
    2003. 32 pp. ISBN 91-7106-508-3

23. Kenneth Good, *Bushmen and Diamonds. (Un) Civil Society in Botswana.*
    2003. 39 pp. ISBN 91-7106-520-2

24. Robert Kappel, Andreas Mehler, Henning Melber and Anders Danielson, *Structural Stability in an African Context.*
    2003. 55 pp. ISBN 91-7106-521-0

25. Patrick Bond, *South Africa and Global Apartheid. Continental and International Policies and Politics.*
    2004. 45 pp. ISBN 91-7106-523-7

26. Bonnie Campbell (ed.), *Regulating Mining in Africa. For whose benefit?*
    2004. 89 pp. ISBN 91-7106-527-X

27. Suzanne Dansereau and Mario Zamponi, *Zimbabwe – The Political Economy of Decline.* Compiled by Henning Melber.
    2005. 43 pp. ISBN 91-7106-541-5

28. Lars Buur and Helene Maria Kyed, *State Recogni-tion of Traditional Authority in Mozambique. The nexus of Community Representation and State Assist-ance.*
2005. 30 pp. ISBN 91-7106-547-4

29. Hans Eriksson and Björn Hagströmer, *Chad – Towards Democratisation or Petro-Dictatorship?*
2005. 82 pp.ISBN 91-7106-549-

30. Mai Palmberg and Ranka Primorac (eds), *Skinning the Skunk – Facing Zimbabwean Futures.*
2005. 40 pp. ISBN 91-7106-552-0

31. Michael Brüntrup, Henning Melber and Ian Taylor, *Africa, Regional Cooperation and the World Market – Socio-Economic Strategies in Times of Global Trade Regimes.* Com-piled by Henning Melber.
2006. 70 pp. ISBN 91-7106-559-8

32. Fibian Kavulani Lukalo, *Extended Handshake or Wrestling Match? – Youth and Urban Culture Celebrating Politics in Kenya.*
2006.58 pp. ISBN 91-7106-567-9

33. Tekeste Negash, *Education in Ethiopia: From Crisis to the Brink of Collapse.*
2006. 55 pp. ISBN 91-7106-576-8

34. Fredrik Söderbaum and Ian Taylor (eds) *Micro-Regionalism in West Africa. Evidence from Two Case Studies.*
2006. 32 pp. ISBN 91-7106-584-9

35. Henning Melber (ed.), *On Africa – Scholars and African Studies.*
2006. 68 pp. ISBN 978-91-7106-585-8

36. Amadu Sesay, *Does One Size Fit All? The Sierra Leone Truth and Reconciliation Commission Revisited.*
2007. 56 pp. ISBN 978-91-7106-586-5

37. Karolina Hulterström, Amin Y. Kamete and Henning Melber, *Political Opposition in African Countries – The Case of Kenya, Namibia, Zambia and Zimbabwe.*
2007. 86 pp. ISBN 978-7106-587-2

38. Henning Melber (ed.), *Governance and State Delivery in Southern Africa. Examples from Botswana, Namibia and Zimbabwe.*
2007. 65 pp. ISBN 978-91-7106-587-2

39. Cyril Obi (ed.), *Perspectives on Côte d'Ivoire: Between Political Breakdown and Post-Conflict Peace.*
2007. 66 pp. ISBN 978-91-7106-606-6

40. Anna Chitando, *Imagining a Peaceful Society. A Vision of Children's Literature in a Post-Conflict Zimbabwe.*
2008. 26 pp. ISBN 978-91-7106-623-7

41. Olawale Ismail, *The Dynamics of Post-Conflict Reconstruction and Peace Building in West Africa. Between Change and Stability.*
2009.52 pp. ISBN 978-91-7106-637-4

42. Ron Sandrey and Hannah Edinger, *Examining the South Africa–China Agricultural Relationship.*
2009. 58 pp. ISBN 978-91-7106-643-5

43. Xuan Gao, *The Proliferation of Anti-Dumping and Poor Governance in Emerging Economies.*
2009. 41 pp. ISBN 978-91-7106-644-2

44. Lawal Mohammed Marafa, *Africa's Business and Development Relationship with China. Seeking Moral and Capital Values of the Last Economic Frontier.*
2009. xx pp. ISBN 978-91-7106-645-9

45. Mwangi wa Githinji, *Is That a Dragon or an Elephant on Your Ladder? The Potential Impact of China and India on Export Led Growth in African Countries.*
2009. 40 pp. ISBN 978-91-7106-646-6

46. Jo-Ansie van Wyk, *Cadres, Capitalists, Elites and Coalitions. The ANC, Business and Development in South Africa.*
2009. 61 pp. ISBN 978-91-7106-656-5

47. Elias Courson, *Movement for the Emancipation of the Niger Delta (MEND). Political Marginalization, Repression and Petro-Insurgency in the Niger Delta.*2009. 30 pp. ISBN 978-91-7106-657-2

48. Babatunde Ahonsi, *Gender Violence and HIV/AIDS in Post-Conflict West Africa. Issues and Responses.* 2010.
38 pp. ISBN 978-91-7106-665-7

49. Usman Tar and Abba Gana Shettima, *Endangered Democracy? The Struggle over Secularism and its Implications for Politics and Democracy in Nigeria.*
2010. 21 pp. ISBN 978-91-7106-666-4

50. Garth Andrew Myers, *Seven Themes in African Urban Dynamics.*2010. 28 pp.
ISBN 978-91-7106-677-0

51. Abdoumaliq Simone, *The Social Infrastructures of City Life in Contemporary Africa.*
2010. 33 pp. ISBN 978-91-7106-678-7

52. Li Anshan, *Chinese Medical Cooperation in Africa. With Special Emphasis on the Medical Teams and Anti-Malaria Campaign.*
2011. 24 pp. ISBN 978-91-7106-683-1

53. Folashade Hunsu, *Zangbeto: Navigating the Spaces Between Oral art, Communal Security And Conflict Mediation in Badagry, Nigeria.*
2011. 27 pp. ISBN 978-91-7106-688-6

54. Jeremiah O. Arowosegbe, *Reflections on the Challenge of Reconstructing Post-Conflict States in West Africa: Insights from Claude Ake's Political Writings.*
2011. 40 pp. ISBN 978-91-7106-689-3

55. Bertil Odén, *The Africa Policies of Nordic Countries and the Erosion of the Nordic Aid Model: A comparative study.*
2011. 66 pp. ISBN 978-91-7106-691-6

56. Angela Meyer, *Peace and Security Cooperation in Central Africa: Developments, Challenges and Prospects.*
2011. 47 pp ISBN 978-91-7106-693-0

57. Godwin R. Murunga, *Spontaneous or Premeditated? Post-Election Violence in Kenya.*
2011. 58 pp. ISBN 978-91-7106-694-7

58. David Sebudubudu & Patrick Molutsi, *The Elite as a Critical Factor in National Development: The Case of Botswana.*
2011. 48 pp. ISBN 978-91-7106-695-4

59. Sabelo J. Ndlovu-Gatsheni, *The Zimbabwean Nation-State Project. A Historical Diagnosis of Identity and Power-Based Conflicts in a Postcolonial State.*
2011. 97 pp. ISBN 978-91-7106-696-1

60. Jide Okeke, *Why Humanitarian Aid in Darfur is not a Practice of the 'Responsibility to Protect'.*
2011. 45 pp. ISBN 978-91-7106-697-8

61. Florence Odora Adong, *Recovery and Development Politics. Options for Sustainable Peacebuilding in Northern Uganda.*
2011, 72 pp. ISBN 978-91-7106-698-5

62. Osita A. Agbu, *Ethnicity and Democratisation in Africa. Challenges for Politics and Development.*
2011, 30 pp. ISBN 978-91-7106-699-2

63. Cheryl Hendricks, *Gender and Security in Africa. An Overview.*
2011, 32 pp. ISBN 978-91-7106-700-5

64. Adebayo O. Olukoshi, *Democratic Governance and Accountability in Africa. In Search of a Workable Framework.*
2011, 25 pp. ISBN 978-91-7106-701-2

65. Christian Lund, *Land Rights and Citizenship in Africa.*
2011, 31 pp. ISBN 978-91-7106-705-0

66. Lars Rudebeck, *Electoral Democratisation in Post-Civil War Guinea-Bissau 1999–2008.*
2011, 31 pp. ISBN 978-91-7106-706-7

67. Kidane Mengisteab, *Critical Factors in the Horn of Africa's Raging Conflicts.*
2011, 39 pp. ISBN 978-91-7106-707-4

68. Solomon T. Ebobrah, *Reconceptualising Democratic Local Governance in the Niger Delta.*
2011, 32 pp. ISBN 978-91-7106-709-8

69. Linda Darkwa, *The Challenge of Sub-regional Security in West Africa. The Case of the 2006 ECOWAS Convention on Small Arms and Light Weapons.*
2011, 39 pp. ISBN 978-91-7106-710-4

www.ingramcontent.com/pod-product-compliance
Ingram Content Group UK Ltd.
Pitfield, Milton Keynes, MK11 3LW, UK
UKHW051652180426
11947UKWH00021B/1912